THE SHOT HEARD ROUND THE WORLD
The Battles of Lexington and Concord

THE SHOT HEARD ROUND THE WORLD
The Battles of Lexington and Concord

Nancy Whitelaw

MORGAN
REYNOLDS
Incorporated

620 South Elm Street Suite 384
Greensboro, North Carolina 27406
http://www.morganreynolds.com

THE SHOT HEARD ROUND THE WORLD:
THE BATTLES OF LEXINGTON AND CONCORD

Cover Illustration: Plate I, The Battle of Lexington *by Amos Doolittle,*
April 19, 1775. Courtesy of the Connecticut Historical
Society, Hartford.
Picture credits: Courtesy of the Library of Congress

The Library of Congress Cataloging-in-Publication Data

Whitelaw, Nancy.
  The shot heard round the world : the battles of Lexington and Concord / Nancy
Whitelaw.-- 1st ed.
    p. cm.
  Includes bibliographical references and index.
  ISBN 1-883846-75-7 (lib. bdg.)
    1. Lexington, Battle of, 1775--Juvenile literature. 2. Concord, Battle of, 1775--Juvenile
literature. [1. Lexington, Battle of, 1775. 2. Concord, Battle of, 1775. 3. United
States--History--Revolution, 1775-1783--Campaigns.] I.Title.

E241.L6 W6 2001
973.3'311--dc21

                                                              00-067567

Printed in the United States of America
First Edition

Dedicated with love to Mary Avery—
a dear friend and fellow essence-hunter

Contents

Chapter One
First Blood 9

Chapter Two
The Trial 15

Chapter Three
The Tea Party 27

Chapter Four
Waiting for War 34

Chapter Five
Spies on Both Sides 49

Chapter Six
Two if by Sea 62

Chapter Seven
Paul Revere's Ride 70

Chapter Eight
On to Concord 80

Chapter Nine
A "Common Hero" 91

Appendix: Famous Leaders 99
Glossary 101
Chapter Notes 103
Bibliography 107
Index 110

The battle on Concord Bridge.

Chapter One

_____

_____

First Blood

Five years before the Revolutionary War began, the first bloodshed occurred in Boston, Massachusetts. It was March 5, 1770.

Around eight o'clock in the evening, British Private Hugh White stood on guard duty in King Street near the Customs House. Although he carried his musket on his shoulder in precise military style, his mind was probably far from that cold, dark night in Boston. Maybe he was thinking about his home and family 3,000 miles away.

"Redcoat!"

"Lobster back!"

Every night, and every day too, it was the same thing: Citizens of Boston taunted the red-coated British guards. Sometimes, it was just a sneering reference to their bright uniforms. Other times, insulting remarks were aimed at all the British soldiers who occupied their city, at the Parliament in London, and at King George III himself. The animosity was so great toward the guards that even little children sneaked up behind them and threw snowballs.

Sometimes the taunting became too much to bear. This is what happened on that fateful night. The jeering remarks were not that unusual, and they were not even addressed to White.

It was Edward Garrick, a Yankee teen, who precipitated the action that led to what would later be called a "massacre." Passing by the guard house, Garrick yelled an insult at one of the guards. Immediately, White took on the duty of reprimanding Garrick for insulting an officer of the crown.

First he shouted at Garrick. Then he approached him and slapped him with his musket. Afterwards, White walked back to his post, and Garrick left the scene.

This might have been the end of what was becoming a common incident in Boston in the 1770s. But instead it was just the beginning. Minutes after he left, Garrick returned to the guard house with a group of young friends. Again, insults flew, followed by threats. As the voices grew louder, more colonists joined the scene. Soon a swearing, jeering mass of several hundred citizens filled the square in front of the Customs House.

"Lobster back! Lobster back!" they chanted over and over at the red-coated soldiers. When shouts were not enough to satisfy their anger, they threw sticks, snowballs, clam shells, and pieces of ice. Church bells tolled, drawing larger and larger crowds into the street. John Adams, a prominent Boston lawyer, later described the scene: "[T]he multitude was shouting and huzzaing and threatening life, the bells ringing, the mob whistling, screaming and rending

Boston, 1776.

like an Indian yell, the people from all quarters throwing every species of rubbish into the streets."

The captain of the guards, Thomas Preston, recognized the imminent danger to his soldiers. He ordered seven of his men to stand in front of the Customs House with bayonets ready. A Boston merchant approached the captain and warned him not to order his troops to fire. Preston did not need that warning. He was well aware of the consequence of British soldiers firing on (probably unarmed) Patriots. Reprimanded and threatened Americans were one thing. Wounded and, God forbid, dead Americans were quite another. His soldiers knew it too. They knew they could be hanged if they fired without orders to do so. The mob sensed Preston's hesitation. They shouted louder, taunting the Redcoats for carrying weapons and not using them.

Then a Patriot threw an icy snowball at a Redcoat. Stunned by the impact, the soldier fell. As he scrambled to his feet, his gun fired. Historians know that he was not given the order to fire, but no one knows if he fired on purpose or if the gun went off accidentally. At the sound of that gunshot, Captain Preston ordered his squad to move through the crowd with lowered bayonets. The Patriots continued to tease and jeer, secure in their belief that the first gunshot was a mistake and that the Redcoats would not fire again.

In a nearby tavern, Crispus Attucks, a young black dock worker, heard the commotion. Looking for action, he encouraged about thirty of his friends to leave the tavern

Paul Revere's engraving of the Boston Massacre.

with him. They carried heavy clubs as they raced to the scene. When they got there, they saw Preston in front of the crowd, probably trying to reason with the mob. Attucks was not interested in reasoning. He hit Preston in the arm with his club. Then he yelled, "Lobster back, I'm going to have one of your claws!" as he hit another Redcoat over the head, knocking him down. The hullabaloo increased with shouts of "Fire! Fire! Fire!" from panicked Redcoats and shouts of "Get the lobsters!" from the Patriots. The guards reached the end of their patience. Fearful that they were in danger of attack, they did not wait for orders. They opened fire on the mob. The crowd rushed backwards, falling over each other, slipping on the hard-packed snow, scrambling to get out of the way of the gunfire.

British soldiers came pouring into the street from quarters all over the city. They stood in disciplined platoons, bayonets ready to resist the mob. Lieutenant Governor Thomas Hutchinson pushed his way through to the balcony of the State House. His goal was to show that he was in control and that justice would be done. He convinced the regiments to go back to their barracks and the citizens to go back to their homes by telling them that there would be a thorough investigation of the incident.

When the streets cleared, five Patriots lay dead or dying. Attucks, with two bullets in his chest, was one of the dead men. Patriots picked the bodies out of the snow and frozen mud and carried them to their homes.

The first blood of the Revolution had been shed.

Chapter Two

The Trial

The first conflicts between the colonists and the British had seemed like family quarrels. Great Britain, the "mother," wanted more authority over the colonists, her "children," who wanted more independence. To quiet the cries for independence, England sent soldiers, tax collectors, and other officials across the Atlantic. To assert their independence, colonists mocked the soldiers, ignored the tax collectors, and defied other officials. The mother country answered with restrictive laws such as the Quartering Act, the Navigation Acts, the Tea Acts, and the Stamp Act. The colonists answered with written petitions, oral protests, and increasingly hostile demonstrations. Like most children, the colonists wanted to retain respect and loyalty to their parent; they just wanted to do it in their own way. The Boston Massacre, as the riot on King Street in May 1770 came to be called, proved the escalation of the growing conflict.

Rumor said that the Boston Massacre was started by Samuel Adams. Bostonians knew that Sam had the kind of mind and spirit to make the posters that had appeared around the city in the earliest days of March. These signs, predicting a British attack on the city, carried signatures of British soldiers. Few colonists doubted that Adams had written the message and faked the signatures. Of course, Sam could not have known for sure the effect the posters would have, but he did know that sooner or later this kind of propaganda would lead to open rebellion.

Samuel Adams, a lawyer and tax collector, was a political activist even before he graduated from Harvard College. In his graduation speech, he had shocked many in the audience by contending that civil disobedience was sometimes necessary.

After graduation, Sam Adams frequently engaged in what he called acts of civil disobedience and what the British eventually called acts of treason. He used threats to make life miserable for British soldiers and officials who tried to exert control over the colonists. He organized the Boston Sons of Liberty, militia who were eager and ready to fight for independence from England. He wrote and distributed what were called "journals": single sheets of anecdotes that condemned the British in Boston. Most of the journal anecdotes, such as the ones about the British beating American children and assaulting colonial women, were partially or completely false. Some of it was true; all of it was inflammatory.

The morning after the Bostonians were fired upon, Sam Adams faced Lieutenant Governor Thomas Hutchinson and

Samuel Adams was a vehement supporter of American independence from Great Britain.

demanded that British soldiers be removed from the streets of Boston. After some stalling, Hutchinson yielded to Adams's demand.

It was probably Sam Adams who coined the term "Boston Massacre" for what others called a riot or simply a demonstration that got out of hand. He insisted that the shootings were a deliberate slaughter. He was persistent in his calls to the colonists to fight against the power of the crown. He cheered as militia formed and drilled in public. "Innocence is no longer safe," he declared. "We are now obliged to appeal to god and our arms for defense."

Although with a different perspective, Sam's cousin John Adams was also deeply involved in the incident on King Street. In fact, he became one of the most important figures in the events after the riot.

John Adams was a lawyer, highly respected for his knowledge of government and law. Socially, he was awkward and self-conscious, a man who believed that people laughed at his roly-poly face and figure. He told a friend, "I have a dread of contempt," and described himself as "stiff and uneasy, ungraceful, and my attention is unsteady and irregular." Despite these feelings, Adams was determined to succeed in life. One day, he wrote in his diary: "I am resolved to rise with the sun and to study the scriptures on Thursday, Friday, Saturday, and Sunday mornings, and to study some Latin author the other 3 mornings . . . May I blush whenever I suffer one hour to pass unimproved." He resolved to speak out for causes and to exert himself to the

Thomas Hutchinson was leuitenant governor of the colony of Massachusetts at the time of the Boston Massacre. He would later be appointed governor.

fullest for these causes. Above all these resolutions, he promised to lead a strictly moral life according to the tenets of the Christian faith. His belief in justice for all was as strong as his religious beliefs. Contrary to the wisdom of the day, Adams declared that the wealthy aristocracy were no better, morally or politically, than the poorer classes.

Until 1765, he was a loyal British subject who wrote proudly of "our British ancestors, who have defended for us the inherent rights of mankind . . ." But when the British announced that the Stamp Act would require colonists to pay even more import taxes to England, Adams objected. From the moment he heard about it, even before it became law, John Adams fought against that act and the authority behind it. He was no longer willing to accept the right of Parliament to tax citizens whom they did not represent. John Adams became an outspoken defender of colonial rights and a defender of rebellion when those rights were threatened.

He joined other Patriots who called themselves the Sons of Liberty. But he had nothing to do with them when they became mobs who seized and destroyed loads of stamped papers. He would never join the Sons of Liberty in their threats that any British official who interfered with their activities would be tarred and feathered. Tarring and feathering was a particularly cruel torture in which boiling tar was poured over the naked victim. Then, the contents of feather pillows were thrown over his body. This act was far from John Adams's view of justice.

This unfortunate tax collector was tarred and feathered. The colonists are pouring tea down his throat.

Adams had heard the commotion as he sat in a social club near King Street. He and his friends rushed to find out what was going on. Although he was a strong supporter of the American rebellion against the British, he had no stomach for street fights. He would do his fighting in a courtroom, not in a brawl. On that fateful day, he sneaked behind the mobs with his mind on his pregnant wife, Abigail, not on the demonstrations. The next day, he accepted the request of one of Preston's friends to defend the captain and six of his soldiers in their upcoming trials for murder.

John Adams was aware that demands for revenge from both sides would only grow louder and more insistent. He asked for a speedy trial to put a resolution to the matter. This did not happen because two of the judges appointed to hear that trial were sick.

The situation might have moved smoothly along to some conciliation except for the strong wills of men like Sam Adams. To him, the shooting that did not become a war instead became both a threat and a challenge. Sam Adams increased his acts of civil disobedience and his attempts to urge others to do the same. He stepped up the pace with the Committees of Correspondence that he had helped organize in 1772, who spread the news of British aggression and colonial defiance from colony to colony. He encouraged the Sons of Liberty to conduct military drills in public. He wrote a 10,000-word letter to Hutchinson denying any authority of the crown over the colonists.

When he learned that Parliament had repealed some of the most onerous customs of the Townshend Acts, Sam Adams refused to accept the British acts of conciliation. He might have encouraged the colonists to drop, or at least minimize, their boycott of British goods. Instead he ranted against the threepence per pound tax on tea and reminded the colonists that they should not accept any taxation by the British until they were represented in the British Parliament. In Sam Adams's mind, anyone who bought a single pound of taxed tea was a traitor to the cause of liberty.

In the fall, the trial of Captain Preston opened. He was tried alone because he had the most authority as the leader of the guard. John Adams defended him. When questioned, British soldiers who had been near Preston in the square swore that he had not given the order to fire. After deliberation, the jury found him innocent.

Next, John Adams defended the six enlisted men who had been arrested with Preston. The jury listened to about five weeks of testimony. They listened to John Adams argue that the British soldiers were not guilty of murder, that they had fired in self-defense. Adams said that it was unreasonable to expect them to stand by passively while they were being attacked. After the testimony, the jury deliberated for about two and a half hours. They returned a verdict of manslaughter for two soldiers on the grounds that they had fired before it was absolutely necessary for their self-defense. These two soldiers were sentenced to a branding of the letter "M" on their thumbs. The jury returned a verdict of innocent for the other four defendants. A few colonists believed that the verdict was just, that the British soldiers had been provoked beyond endurance. Most colonists disagreed with the jury's decision and felt angrier and more vengeful than they had when the incident occurred.

Repercussions from the incident continued. Among those most disturbed by the verdict were Paul Revere and Sam Adams. Paul Revere, an engraver and silversmith, was one of those Patriots who wanted to keep the riot strong in the hearts and minds of colonists. He engraved a drawing of the incident which he titled "The Bloody Massacre." He ignored some of the truth about what happened. He depicted a British officer ordering his troops to fire on unarmed Patriots; he labeled the Customs House the "Butcher's Hall." This engraving became immediately popular and remains so today.

Sam Adams did not give the people of Boston the opportunity to forget the unfortunate incident. He kept up a steady stream of newspaper articles, often written under a pseudonym, retelling and often exaggerating the events of March 5. As a key figure in the creation of the Committees of Correspondence in each of the colonies, he now used this networking to replay incidents of the so-called massacre and to make dire predictions about the future.

But as the months passed, memories of the shooting on King Street faded, as did the outrage against the threepence tax on tea. Colonists enjoyed their daily tea, and even with

Lawyer John Adams successfully defended British Captain Preston and six soldiers who participated in the Boston Massacre.

the import tax, prices were cheaper on the open market than on the black market. Sam Adams's ranting and raving lost its bite. He had warned them of direct British attacks, of the loss of all their freedoms, of the imposition of martial law. Over a year had passed since that first bloodshed on King Street, and still there was no war or martial law. The dire prophecies had not come true. So much for Sam Adams and his rabble-rousing Sons of Liberty.

Then once again, a period of relative tranquility between the colonies and the mother country was shattered by the actions of a rash leader. Three thousand miles away, newly appointed Prime Minister Lord Frederick North attempted to help the powerful East India Company avoid bankruptcy. His plan was to eliminate all middlemen in the selling of tea and to give the monopoly on American sales to the East India Company. North's plan was to have the company include the tax in the wholesale price of tea. The tea would be cheaper in America despite the tax because no middlemen in either country would get a cut. North thought that because it was hidden in the price most colonists would not realize that they were paying a tax. He was wrong.

ChapterThree

The Tea Party

Prime Minister North had not foreseen that American middlemen, such as John Hancock, would object to being shut out of the lucrative tea business. Hancock, who ran a highly successful import-export business, was well known in Boston, not just because he wore fashionable wigs, red velvet breeches, and blue and gold coats with jeweled buttons and lace trim. He was also well known for his economic views. He became involved with the Sons of Liberty and other Patriot groups when British customs threatened his business. Part of the reason that he was one of the richest men in New England was that he avoided paying customs. He would bring in goods in incorrectly labeled boxes and barrels, unload late at night or early in the morning, or simply ignore the required paperwork. When apprehended for smuggling, he and his workers were masters at bribery. For example, they could convince customs workers not to collect any tax on molasses by simply offering them a bribe of a penny and a half on each gallon. Hancock would still make money on the molasses.

When he was elected a selectman of Boston in 1765,

Hancock encouraged Bostonians to protest against the crown. He added, "I hope the same spirit will prevail throughout the whole continent."

In 1767, customs officials had seized his ship, *Liberty,* on charges that the crew had unloaded about 3,000 gallons of Madeira wine in twenty-five casks without paying customs. The *Liberty* was towed from the wharf and anchored close to the British ship *Romney.* The wine somehow disappeared, and Hancock never got his ship back.

Bostonians listened when Hancock spoke and watched when he went by. He was known for spending money as well as acquiring it. People gawked at him when he drove by in a yellow carriage wearing a lavender suit, an ornate wig, and shiny buttons, belts, and buckles. He entertained high society in his magnificent mansion with ornate furniture, magnificent gardens, and an invaluable artwork collection. Hancock also gave away money. He gave a fire engine to Boston, steeples to churches, firewood to the poor. Occasionally he hosted parties for poor people, feasts on Boston Common with roasted oxen and casks of rum for all. Some of his admirers followed his chariot through the streets shouting "Squire Hancock" and even "King Hancock." If Lord North's actions threatened Hancock, the citizens of Boston would stand behind their idol.

Another repercussion that Lord North did not anticipate was the colonists' recognition of the threat of a government-imposed monopoly. In the immediate future, that monopoly would put American tea wholesalers and retailers out of work. Later, that monopoly on tea might be

Businessman John Hancock was one of the richest men in New England.

extended to a monopoly on cloth, wine, shoes, or any other imported item.

Sam Adams was back in stride, and the Sons of Liberty sprang to attention. Posters all around town announced meetings and demonstrations of protest. In the ports of New York and Philadelphia, crowds waving clubs and throwing paving stones kept tea ships from dropping anchor. Some Patriot soldiers called themselves minutemen, telling the other colonists that they were ready to fight at a minute's notice. Once again, the words "taxation without representation" became a rallying cry for action against the crown. It became increasingly obvious on both sides of the Atlantic that North's actions and the colonists' reactions could lead to a revolutionary war.

Strengthened by the response of the colonists, Sam Adams again went after Governor Hutchinson, who was now the governor of Massachusetts. In a circular letter sent to all the colonies, he criticized Hutchinson for accepting a change in his relationship to the colonists. Hutchinson had agreed with Parliament that his salary would no longer be paid by the colonies. Instead it would be paid by the crown. Adams pointed out to the readers of his letter that this would allow the crown to control the actions of the governor.

More than two years had passed since the first blood of the revolution had been shed. Now the conflict was building again. As the tea ship the *Dartmouth* plied its way across the Atlantic in November 1773, officials on both sides of the ocean agreed that the impending crisis might result in all-out war. Citizens gathered around the Liberty Tree, so-named because it was often used as a center for broadsides against the British. Tacked on the tree was an announcement calling Patriots to meet at Faneuil Hall at nine o'clock "to make united and successful resistance to this last, worst, and most destructive measure of Administration." This was a reference to the attempt to import tea against colonial wishes. Thanks to Sam Adams, a copy of this message was sent to neighboring towns as well as to the Committees of Correspondence in each colony.

Sam Adams took the stage at the meeting. He told the 5,000 assembled citizens that they should send a message to the captain of the *Dartmouth* to tie up at Griffin's Wharf and not to unload his cargo. Adams called for another meeting the next morning, where the colonists decided to send Paul Revere to warn neighboring sea ports that the tea ships might sail out of Boston harbor to unload at other cities.

Two more tea ships joined the *Dartmouth* at Griffin's Wharf. In all, the ships carried 342 chests of tea, a cargo worth about 18,000 British pounds. Sam Adams urged the citizens to vote to send the ships back to England without being unloaded. If this vote had been taken at a regular town meeting, only Boston property holders would be allowed to vote. But Sam set no requirements for voting. Even women were allowed to shout aye or nay when the vote was called. It was rumored that he recruited many "temporary Bostonians" from neighboring towns. The result of the vote was a loud and determined "Aye."

Governor Hutchinson sent a speedy answer. If the tea was not unloaded by dock workers by December 17, customs officials would do the unloading. Then they would auction it off to any buyers who agreed to pay the duties. The implications of this plan were obvious to Sam Adams and the others. In order to prevent the unloading, Patriots would have to attack customs officials, creating an encounter which might well lead to war.

Sam faced the crowd. "This meeting can do nothing more to save the country," he declared. Those words were a prepared signal. Scarcely a minute later, war whoops erupted from the back of the room. No one knows exactly how many men (estimations vary from 30 to 150) suddenly appeared, disguised with face paint and costumes to look like Mohawk Indians. The "Mohawks" invited the audience to accompany them to the pier.

The harbor front resounded with cheers, jeers, threats, and terms of triumph. The "Indians" boarded the ships, broke open all 342 chests with their tomahawks, and threw about 35,000 pounds of tea into the harbor. Less than three hours later, they marched victoriously (still disguised) through the streets of Boston, accompanied by fife and drum. The "Boston Tea Party" had been all its planners had hoped for and more, not just for Bostonians but also for other colonists. Both New York and Pennsylvania greeted the news of the Boston Tea Party with glee and vowed to do the same if British cargo ships entered their ports.

News of the Boston Tea Party reached London in late

Dressed as Mohawk Indians, Patriots dumped British tea into Boston Harbor in defiance of taxation without representation.

January of 1774. Citizens and officials alike greeted the news first with shock and then with outrage. There was nearly unanimous agreement that the colonists would have to pay dearly for this offense. King George and Lord North met with General Thomas Gage, who happened to be in London at the time. Maybe Gage did not truly understand the situation, or maybe he was merely telling the king what he wanted to hear. In any case, the general said that the colonists did not pose a serious threat to the crown. Because Gage was the commander-in-chief of British forces in America, his words were believed. But when the General returned to America, the tone of his reports would be radically different.

Chapter Four

Waiting for War

In the reports he began sending back to London after he returned to Massachusetts, Gage expressed fear of open, perhaps imminent, rebellion. Lord North took immediate action. He announced to members of Parliament that they must stand firm: "convince your colonies that you are . . . not afraid to control them, and depend on it, obedience will be the result of your deliberations." Most British officials believed North when he told them that strict regulation of the Massachusetts colony would serve as a threat to all the other colonies. North devised what became known as the Coercive Acts against Massachusetts.

The Coercive Acts closed the port of Boston, forbade the legislature and courts to meet, prohibited town meetings, re-instated mandated quartering of British troops in private homes of the citizens of Massachusetts, and imposed military rule. Gage declared that the port of Boston would be re-opened only after the colonists paid reparations for the tea destroyed in the Boston Tea Party. As soon as the Coercive Acts were announced in Boston, Patriots disseminated the news to the Committees of Correspondence in the other colonies.

As soon as the committee in South Carolina heard that the port of Boston was closed, they sent money and rice. When the committee in Pennsylvania heard this, they sent flour. Long Islanders sent 100 sheep. The success of the Committees of Correspondence led a British supporter, or a Loyalist, to describe the members of these committees as "the foulest, subtlest, and most venomous serpent ever issued from the egg of sedition."

All this was too much for Massachusetts Governor Hutchinson, who had for months been trying to resign with a good pension. When he finally convinced officials in London that they should let him resign, General Gage became governor, still holding his title of commander. This elevation of a military man to governor indicated that the British were serious about maintaining martial law in the colony. This in turn stiffened the colonists' resistance to the authority of the crown.

Patriots encouraged demonstrations in every village and city to urge the overthrow of the Coercive Acts, which they were now calling the Intolerable Acts. Dock workers in Philadelphia, New York, and several other ports continued to refuse to unload cargo. Aware that many Loyalists were spies for the crown, Patriots strengthened their own spy network among the colonies.

Sam Adams encouraged his fellow citizens not to fight against the Intolerable Acts. He urged them to endure the embargo as an act of loyalty to the principles in which they believed. He told them: "Our oppressors cannot force us into submission by reducing us to a state of starvation . . . The real wants and necessitates of man are few."

The First Continental Congress met in September 1774. Sam Adams wanted to prepare the colonies to unite in rebellion and, if necessary, in war against the British. The congress divided into two groups on this question. The leaders of one group were Joseph Galloway and John Dickinson of Philadelphia, who wanted to mediate a solution with the king. The leaders of the other group were Samuel and John Adams of Massachusetts, Charles Thomson of Pennsylvania, and Patrick Henry of Virginia. These men wanted to declare total independence from the crown if England did not immediately yield to the Patriot demands to repeal the acts. When some delegates warned that talk of independence from Britain was treason, Patrick Henry answered, "If this be treason, make the most of it!" A vote was taken. The plan to mediate was defeated. Hardliners like Sam Adams dominated the meeting from that time on.

One basic problem was to unite the two million citizens of the thirteen colonies. The colonies filled a territory 1,500 miles long and several hundred miles wide. Delegates voted for an immediate end to all trade with Great Britain. They printed a document entitled *Declaration and Resolves,* which denied Parliament any power to enact legislation affecting the colonies. Sam Adams urged the

This British parody depicts Bostonians held captive in a Liberty Tree. The fish represent provisions sent by other colonies after the port of Boston was closed.

representatives to alert the colonists of a possible attack from British military forces.

While the First Continental Congress was meeting in Philadelphia, towns in Massachusetts elected delegates to another meeting of the Massachusetts Provincial Congress. This body would take the place of the Massachusetts House that was dissolved earlier. In the first meetings, the congress passed three crucial votes. One was to send no more duties or taxes of any kind to England. Another was to set up militia companies of fifty privates and the necessary officers. A third vote established groups called Committees of Safety to speed communications and cooperation among the colonies.

At town meetings in Boston and the surrounding area, people discussed the need for militia and for arms, and many towns voted to tax themselves to pay for wagons for hauling cannon, for gathering and storing ammunition, and for drums and fifes for military bands. Townspeople brought guns to central locations, ready to use or to lend as the need might arise. Most of these guns were designed for hunting—matchlocks and flintlocks that required pans of priming powder, muskets which were accurate at about 100 yards, and a few long-barreled rifles.

Throughout the winter of 1774-75, Patriots formed militias of minutemen and drilled regularly. Some soldiers were veterans of the French and Indian War, and these veterans served as drill leaders. Militiamen had no uniforms. Most wore their everyday homespun business and

"If this be treason, make the most of it!" declared the outspoken Patrick Henry.

farming clothes. They had no military arms either, so they carried hunting weapons.

It was not just uniforms that distinguished the Redcoats from the Yankee militia. The Redcoats, called Regulars, were professional soldiers who had chosen the military as a career. Many, if not all, had accepted a military career because they had failed to obtain and keep a job as a civilian. Their lives were full of never-ending discomfort and discipline. The red uniform jackets, which at first glance seemed so grand, were made of heavy, itchy wool. Soldiers were required to wear the same uniforms in both summer and winter. A stiff leather collar, worn to force straight posture, often rubbed soldiers' necks raw. The fancy white breeches were so tight that they sometimes cut off blood circulation in the legs. The Regular's average marching load was about 125 pounds. A soldier's pay was seldom enough to meet personal needs, much less the needs of a family. Torture was a common method of discipline.

On the other side, minutemen were citizen-soldiers. Every able-bodied male colonist between sixteen and sixty-five was required to belong to a militia. Officers were respectful to the men under them. Militiamen drilled only several times a year. After this service, they could enlist if they wished, or they were free to return home until the next announced drill. Outwardly they were civilians, but in their hearts and minds they were soldiers fighting for a cause.

Many towns maintained training fields where the militia drilled in public view. British officers watched these drills

Lord North planned to set an example for the rest of the colonies by punishing Massachusetts after the Boston Tea Party.

and sneered. One British observer wrote: "It is a curious masquerade scene to see grave sober citizens, barbers and tailors who never looked fierce before, strutting about in their Sunday wigs with muskets on their shoulders . . ."

The British were not the only ones who disapproved of the increasing strength of the militias. Some colonists opposed any kind of rebellion against British rule. Some wanted above all to remain loyal English subjects. This conflict among Loyalists and Patriots grew as did conflict between the Patriots and the British.

The early spring of 1775 became an agonizing wait for both Patriots and supporters of the crown. As each side may have wanted to engage in armed conflict, neither group wanted to make the first move.

General Gage impatiently awaited orders from London and tried to maintain an appearance of control. Deserters created a double problem for him. Desertion not only decreased his numbers, but it also put spies in the enemy camp. Many deserters openly supported the Patriots, and Paul Revere and others were delighted to rid them of their red coats and furnish them with farmers' smocks.

Massachusetts Patriots set up a network of spies that met regularly at the Green Dragon Tavern on Union Street in Boston. They were a diverse group of servants, dockhands, tradesmen, doctors, and lawyers. Nobody knows for sure the names of the colonists who met in a private room in that tavern. And nobody knows how many times they met or how much conflict they faced among themselves as they tried to

General Thomas Gage was the commander-in-chief of British forces in America at the start of the Revolutionary War.

deal with the conflict with Great Britain. They could not keep records because the plans they made were no less than treason, a charge punishable by death. But historians do know that some of the plans that led to the revolution were created in that tavern, recognized by the copper dragon on an iron post which decorated the front. Somehow, Governor Gage learned about the meetings, giving rise to the speculation that his American-born wife was a Patriot at heart and perhaps knew someone who attended the meetings.

Gage was confused about the political situation in the colonies, and his messages to Parliament showed this confusion. At first, he sent the message that he did not expect the conflicts to become a war. However, he said, if war should become necessary, the British could easily defeat the colonists. In that case, he was determined to demonstrate to the so-called Patriots for once and for all that they were now and would always remain subjects of King George III. They were indebted to the British government for their very existence in the New World, and they were dependent on Parliament for their political and economic lives. No band of rag-tag soldiers, fancy-tongued orators, or violence-prone citizens could effect a change in the relationship between the mother country of England and her colonial children.

About a month after sending a report showing confidence in the situation, Gage sent a warning of an imminent uprising and asked for 20,000 men to suppress it. He added

General Gage's troops stationed themselves on Boston Common, in front of John Hancock's lavish home (upper right).

that British soldiers were deserting more and more frequently, and that many of these deserters might support the colonies in case of war. King George III was not as confused as Gage. He predicted that "blows must decide whether they are to be subject to the Country or independent." Lord William Dartmouth, successor to Viscount Hillsborough as head of the American Department, drafted a long letter to General Gage, telling him to take strong steps against the rebellion in Massachusetts. "[F]orce should be repelled by force," he commanded.

In England, most citizens and government officials alike expected war with the colonists. Lord North wavered. He proposed that the king send a special commission to America to discuss and resolve disputes. King George III rejected any attempts at negotiation. North continued attempts at a peaceful resolution through secret meetings of high British officials with the colonial agent Benjamin Franklin. The men drafted a document which addressed the needs of both sides. If these suggestions were followed, the Americans would continue to maintain a strong economic and social bond with the crown, while creating a state independent of British authority. The House of Lords, the upper house of the British Parliament, rejected the document.

Parliament voted to convict at least one Patriot of treason, hoping that the punishment of this one colonist would serve as an example to other rebels. Members of Parliament asked the Loyalists in America to send evidence of treason strong enough to support a conviction. Hutchinson chose Sam Adams as the first American traitor to be tried by the crown. An attorney general in London was ordered to thoroughly research the case against Adams. At this point, the crown could not afford a political defeat in a treason trial. When the attorney general expressed doubts that the crown would win in a case against Adams, the idea was dropped.

That fall, when representatives of the General Court were forbidden by the British to convene, they met anyway.

King George III was prepared to fight to keep the American colonies.

They called themselves a provincial congress and assumed all the authority they would have had as a legislature. Under the chairmanship of John Hancock, they called for an army of 30,000, half the soldiers to come from Massachusetts and the other half from New Hampshire, Connecticut, and Rhode Island.

Perhaps the congress was reacting to rumors from London that the British were about to take drastic steps to control the colonies. That rumor did not include a description of the steps, but the colonists assumed that they would be punished, severely restricted, or even attacked. Sam Adams advised his fellow delegates, " 'Put your enemy in the wrong, and keep him so,' is a wise maxim in politics, as well as in war."

Patriots met more frequently. Secret meetings, such as those at the Green Dragon, were held more often. These tavern meetings did not attract the attention of even the most curious British soldiers on duty in that area of Boston. What was the harm in these tradesmen, lawyers, farmers, and businessmen going out for a little drink, maybe a snack, and good friendship to while away the evening hours? Yes, they would talk politics there, but so what? It was no secret that most colonists resented the presence of the British military. It was no secret that some of them were bold enough to criticize King George III and his Parliament. But what could they accomplish in a tavern?

What could they accomplish? As winter warmed to spring in 1775, the possibilities grew and grew and grew.

Chapter Five

Spies on Both Sides

Some of these men in the Green Dragon Tavern were not just looking for refreshment and companionship. They were looking for ways to distance themselves from the British government and to take over some of the responsibilities of governing themselves.

In a private room, these determined men began every meeting with each person swearing on the Bible that he would not reveal anything that was said. Because of this tight security, no one knows the names of all those involved. It has been verified that John Hancock and Sam and John Adams were there.

Sam Adams told anyone who would listen that Parliament was overstepping its authority in taxing imports and exports. He said, "If our Trade be taxed, why not our Lands? Why not the Produce of our Lands & everything we possess or make use of?" What could the colonists do? They were, above all, British citizens loyal to the king and to Parliament just as their ancestors were. Yet Adams spoke the truth. There should be no taxation without representation.

And if they accepted this tax burden now, who knows what further burdens the crown would impose?

Citizens individually and in small groups fought a kind of guerilla warfare. The Sons of Liberty brawled with the Redcoats in taverns. People walking along the streets picked quarrels with the troops. Little children sneaked behind the Regulars to throw snowballs at them.

In February 1775, Parliament came close to declaring war on the colonies, and then they backed away. Instead of a state of war, they declared that Massachusetts was in a state of rebellion. They increased British military presence in the Boston area with a fleet of twenty-nine ships bearing a total of 196 guns.

The very next month, two more near-crises arose. The first was over a colonial printer, Isaiah Thomas, who distributed many flyers, some of which accused Gage of immorality, alcoholism, and other vices. Although the accusations were untrue, the pamphlets had the effect of further rousing Bostonians against all Redcoats in their city. Gage sent messages to England telling of the slander against him. These messages so angered the British that they threatened to tar and feather Thomas if he printed any more propaganda. The crisis faded when Thomas fled to Watertown, New York.

The second near-crisis occurred on the day of the fifth anniversary of the Boston Massacre. Suspense filled the air. Would General Gage allow the annual remembrance of the bloodshed of that day? Would he allow any Patriot

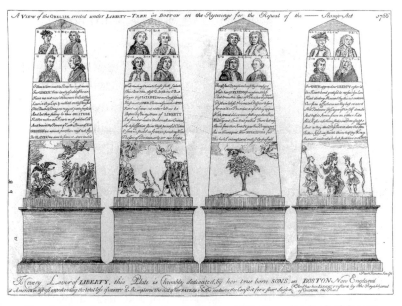

The obelisk under the Liberty Tree in Boston, 1766. Engraving by Paul Revere.

leader to speak in public? Would he simply wait until the crowds had gathered and then arrest them all at once? Patriots crowded into the Old South Church early, unwilling to let the day go unnoticed.

They were not alone; British officers in their bright scarlet coats also filed in. Sam Adams greeted the Redcoats politely, offering them the best seats "so they might have no pretence to behave ill..." Then Sam Adams, John Hancock, and other Patriot leaders sat in the deacons' seats on the raised platform at the front of the church. Dr. Joseph Warren, a Patriot who had proven his loyalty to the cause of independence even before the Boston Massacre, held the audience spellbound with his tirade against George III and

Parliament: "I glory in publicly avowing my eternal enmity to tyranny; and here suffer me to ask with tenderness, what regard the rulers of Great Britain manifested in their late transactions . . ." Another Patriot spoke calmly about the importance of remembering the Boston Massacre, being careful not to offend the British in the audience. Then Sam Adams voted that they plan the next year's celebration.

In protest, British officers chanted "Fie! Fie!" which was misinterpreted as "Fire, Fire." The crowds swarmed out of the building. After much confusion on the part of both British and Americans, order was restored, and the Patriots dispersed. Afterward, a story about Sam Adams and the anniversary memorial passed from Patriot to Patriot with cheers and jokes. The story stated that British officials had practiced a plan to capture Sam Adams and probably some other Patriots at a given signal. That signal was to be a soldier throwing an egg into Dr. Warren's face. Unfortunately for the British, the soldier entrusted with that responsibility supposedly slipped on his way to the meeting and broke the egg.

Gage wanted desperately to subdue the Patriots and to do it quickly and decisively. He knew that every day he postponed confrontation was a day in which the Patriots were readying themselves for the attack. He had threatened and threatened and threatened to no avail. He had faced many problems in carrying out his threat. His troops were cold, hungry, and plagued with an infectious disease that may have been a form of typhus. They were bored and

"I glory in publicly avowing my eternal enmity to tyranny," declared Dr. Joseph Warren.

restless and easily succumbed to the insults and jeers of the Patriots who stood across from them in the Boston Common and harassed them. As morale declined, Gage doubled the guard around Boston, partly to prevent his own men from deserting. He tried to build troop discipline and morale by drilling twice a day on the Common, allowing sessions of target practice in Boston Harbor, and performing relentless inspections of uniforms and equipment, but troop morale fell even more.

Gage found the opportunity to make a positive statement, and to raise the morale of his troops, when he learned that the Patriots were stockpiling munitions and other battle supplies in Concord, Massachusetts. Perhaps he had found the records of militia commander Colonel James Barrett who recorded supplies including 20,000 pounds of musket balls and cartridges and 35,000 pounds of rice. Gage planned a surprise march in April to seize the supplies, keep what he could use, and destroy the rest. He also planned to arrest Patriot leaders Sam Adams and John Hancock. They would be tried for treason and, Gage was sure, be found guilty. He believed that when the colonists learned how Adams and Hancock would be punished— perhaps by hanging, perhaps by drawing and quartering— they would disband their committees and begin behaving like loyal British citizens.

In preparation, he sent two of his best spies, Lieutenant Colonel Frances Smith and Private John Howe, to scout the situation in Concord. Smith and Howe disguised themselves as Yankee working men with gray coats, leather breeches, and silk handkerchiefs around their necks. They told every Patriot they met that they were looking for work. Smith was not able to deceive the Patriots. He was quickly spotted as a British soldier, and he had to give up spying. Howe continued to hunt for jobs, asking for work as a gunsmith and saying that he wanted to help the rebels get ready for the fight to come. In Concord, he got a job repairing guns.

Then, on the pretext of needing to go to his home to get his tools, Howe left for Maine, where he gave British officials specific information about the location and contents of the Patriot stores of munitions. He told Gage that he thought the rebels were determined to be free or to die. Gage eagerly accepted the information about weapons, but he did not foresee serious problems for his troops. He saw the rebels as farmers and not as soldiers, no matter how strong their determination. That is, he saw most of the colonists as farmers, but not John and Samuel Adams or John Hancock and a few others. Gage could recite the names of revolutionaries as easily as he could recite the names of the former kings of England.

It was almost five years after the Boston Massacre when spies told Gage that both Sam Adams and John Hancock would be staying with Hancock's relatives in Lexington while they prepared to attend the Second Continental Congress. Gage had also learned about Concord, twelve miles up the road from Lexington, and the stores of a large supply of muskets and cannon, barrels of gunpowder, bullets, tents, medicines, and food. He knew that with every passing day the colonists were better prepared to meet a British offensive and, perhaps, to mount an offensive of their own. He decided to make his boldest move yet against the Patriots. His men would stop first at Lexington to arrest Sam Adams and Hancock. Then the Redcoats would march on to Concord to capture the munitions and other supplies.

Gage knew that the Patriots were preparing to defend themselves. But he was ignorant of the extent of their preparations and the expertise of their spy network. He was unaware that on April 7, 1775, word was whispered through the colonies that British soldiers were ready to make their boldest move so far.

At that point, the Patriots could only guess at the place and date of the British attack. Concord seemed a likely place, since munitions were stored there and it was within a couple of hours of Boston. The first two weeks in April seemed to be a likely time since spies had overheard snatches of conversation about this period. The date April 9 had been mentioned more than other dates. With this in mind, the Patriots prepared to defend Concord against seizure of supplies on April 9. They sent out the word for miles around Concord that the minutemen should keep their guns ready and be prepared to march at a moment's notice. In Concord itself, men and boys were busy hiding flour, cannon, and bullets. They hauled some supplies by ox carts to what they hoped would be safe areas. They hid others in the swamps. Sam Adams and John Hancock packed a trunk with papers which, if found by the British, would seal their fate as rebels guilty of treason. This trunk would have to be hidden carefully.

Assuming that they had guessed correctly that the target would be Concord, two questions remained for the Boston Patriots. Would the date be April 9, and if not, what would it be? How would the British proceed from Boston to Concord? Increased British activity in the harbor suggested that they would start by crossing the Charles River and go by foot from there. But the increased activity might be a ruse. Maybe the British would march around Back Bay and then continue overland to Concord.

With either plan, carefully positioned spies in Boston probably could not determine the route until the Regulars moved. The problem was that surely the town of Boston would be surrounded with British soldiers the minute the Regulars started their march to Concord. Colonial spies would know the proposed route by then, but they would be stopped before they could leave the town to spread the alarm. Patriot leaders called on a man who had many times proven his dedication to the cause, his bravery, and his skill at riding. That man was Paul Revere. No one could find out for sure, but it was suspected that he had been a "Mohawk" at the Boston Tea Party, and that he had been a messenger in many incidents where early warnings had enabled Patriots to hide supplies from British soldiers. Now Revere served the Patriot cause by figuring out a scheme to spread the alarm once the colonists knew the route of the British.

This was the plan: As soon as Revere learned the route of the British, he would go to the Old North Church where Robert Newman awaited him. He would give Newman information about the route and then rush out of Boston as fast as he could to spread the alarm throughout the countryside. As soon as Newman had the information, he would send the message by lighting lanterns in the steeple. Revere told Newman that "if the British went out by water we would show two lanterns in the North Church steeple—and if by land one as a signal . . ." As sexton of the church, Newman was the perfect man for this job. He had keys to the church, and he lived right across the street from it.

April 9 came and went with no sign of a British offensive. The people of Boston and Concord continued to wait, more anxious each passing day. In the minds of the British and colonists alike, a revolutionary war was inevitable. On April 15, Patriot spies learned that Gage had sent orders to eleven regiments to cease their regular duties. Both sides continued to wait.

Sam Adams's friends had frequently warned him that he could be seized at any moment, thrown onto a British ship, and taken to England to stand trial for treason and incitement to rebellion. Gage would have loved to do this, but he feared that Adams's fellow Americans would react instantly, and that their reaction would lead to violence and bloodshed. Of course, once open violence had occurred, Gage would lose nothing by arresting either Adams or

Paul Revere, an engraver and silversmith, rode from Boston to Concord and Lexington to spread the word that the British were on the march.

Hancock. In fact, he believed he could find justification for his soldiers if either Hancock or Adams were shot dead as soon as they were captured. Patriots were able to persuade both men to flee from Boston. While hating to miss anything, the men had to agree that they would be of more use to the cause as free men than as captives of the crown— or dead.

Within a few days, a Patriot waiter in a tavern overheard British soldiers boasting about some secret plans. A spy who lived on the waterfront brought news that British sailors were repairing their longboats. A servant for a Redcoat overheard talk of British soldiers being put on alert.

On April 17, Sam Adams and John Hancock left the Boston area for Lexington, hoping to escape detection by the British. On that same day, a group of British officers gathered at their stables preparing their horses for a secret mission. In their excitement at the prospect of a battle, they became careless as they talked about the attack to come. They did not know that a Patriot spy, posing as a groom, heard the news and passed it on to Paul Revere as fast as he could.

Spies were watching at noon the next day as British sailors moved the sixty-four-gun warship *Somerset* into the mouth of the Charles River in Boston. They heard the squealing of heavy tackle as crewmen lowered the longboats from the deck of the *Somerset* and moored them under the prow of the ship. That same afternoon, other spies saw small groups of British soldiers traveling from Boston Neck along the road to Concord. These Regulars moved at a leisurely pace, seemingly just out for a walk, but their full uniform dress and the outline of pistols under their long coats told a different story. As the day wore on, dozens of British soldiers strode up and down Boston's Long Wharf, a pier that extended far into the waters of the bay. Others marched to the Common, as Patriots watched and waited.

Chapter Six

Two if by Sea

At nine o'clock on the night of April 18, 1775, British sergeants crept into the Boston Barracks where their troops were sleeping. They whispered orders to don battle gear in silence and in darkness. Moments later, heavy boots scraped on cobblestones as about 700 Redcoats followed their leaders through the dark streets to Boston Common. As silently as possible and with only the light of the full yellow moon, they piled into the longboats waiting in the shadow of the sixty-four-gun British warship *Somerset*. Twelve men could just fit into one of the boats if they all stood up for the short ride across the Charles River. Few boats made it all the way across. The weight of the men plus their sixty-pound packs proved to be too much for the small boats. Before they reached the shore, the soldiers had to drop over the sides and wade the rest of the way in the waist-deep water and muck holding their muskets high to keep them dry. The ferries plied their way back empty and returned full of men, over and over again for two hours. Wet, cold, and nervous, the soldiers waited and waited and waited.

After the last ferry load of soldiers disembarked, British Colonel Francis Smith distributed the rations—so called "ship's biscuits," rock-hard and occasionally infested with maggots. Then Smith lined up the men and they began their twelve-mile trek to Lexington, squishing muddy water from their heavy boots with every step.

Around the time that the first ferryboat had started across the Charles, Dr. Joseph Warren received a secret message. Historians are not sure who sent that message, but it must have been someone with close ties to the Regulars. Perhaps it was a Mrs. Stedman, who, because of the Quartering Act, had a British soldier living in her home. When Gage's sergeant arrived with the orders to prepare to cross the river, the soldier was not at home. The sergeant asked Mrs. Stedman to give him the message to be at the Common that evening ready to march to Concord. As soon as the sergeant left, Mrs. Stedman may have sent the message to a Patriot leader. The news was passed from Patriot to Patriot. The message reported that the Regulars were on the march to Concord. They would cross the Charles River and then head for Concord through Lexington that very night. Warren sent for Revere and for William Dawes, a young shoemaker and fierce rebel.

Warren told Revere that his first task was to alert Newman at the Old North Church as they had planned. Then he had to somehow sneak his rowboat past the *Somerset* and ride on to Lexington. Dawes's responsibility was to head for Concord immediately by way of the Neck. Both men were to alert the townsfolk to be prepared to defend themselves and to warn Adams and Hancock of their impending arrest.

Revere's first destination would be Lexington, about twelve miles away, and then on to Concord, about six miles farther. His mission was to alert the Patriots all along his route that the British Regulars were headed through Lexington to Concord. Patriots should know that the Regulars did not intend to leave the area until they captured the large store of Patriot ammunition in Concord and arrested the Americans Sam Adams and John Hancock for treason.

There was no assurance that either Revere or Dawes would be able to carry out their missions before being caught by the British. Maybe Dawes had the better chance of fooling any British officer who stopped him. Dawes was a talented actor who had many times become a drunken farmer when stopped by the British. Each time the Redcoats had quickly set him free, convinced that no drunken person could be an effective spy. But the disguise might not work this time. He may have looked innocent with his slow-jogging horse and his large floppy hat, but the Regulars were on heightened alert. Revere did not attempt a disguise, although he knew that his strong, stocky build and homespun clothes were familiar to British officials. The three Patriots—Warren, Dawes, and Revere—knew that they would be accused of treason if caught. No loyal British soldier would hesitate to shoot any or all three of the men on sight.

William Dawes, a shoemaker, helped Paul Revere alert Patriots that a British assault was near.

Revere left Warren and sped to the Old North Church to give Newman the message that the British would come by sea. Newman was waiting outside the church. He had pretended to go to bed, slipped out of an upstairs window, crawled along a roof, and then jumped down to the sidewalk to await orders. Revere told him and his friend John Pullings to hang two lanterns in the steeple on the side facing Charlestown. Revere then left quickly, headed for home to prepare for the rest of the evening. He would need spurs and boots, a heavy coat, and something with which to muffle his oars.

Newman grabbed the two small square metal lanterns that he had hidden earlier in a church closet. He and Pullings made their way up the 154 creaky wooden steps past eight large bells to the highest window in the belfry. At the top of the stairs, they took out their flints and sent a stream of sparks into a nest of dry tinder. They blew on the tinder until they had a flame. Then they lit the candles in the lanterns. They climbed to the top window of the steeple, threw open the sash and held both lanterns out in the direction of Charlestown just for a moment. They could only hope that the moment was long enough to send the message to the Patriots and short enough not to arouse the attention of the Regulars on the *Somerset*.

The Patriots in Charlestown received the message. Some hastened to get a horse ready for Revere. One started off for Lexington to warn Hancock and Adams. Others galloped off to alert the people of Cambridge.

Revere reached his home on North Square safely in spite of the increasing numbers of Redcoats heading for the Common. Once inside the house, Revere quickly put on his heavy coat and riding boots. Then he rushed outside again. At a bank of the Charles River, Patriots Thomas Richardson and Joshua Bentley were waiting to row him across to North Boston, where he would find his horse. Legends have grown up about what happened next. One story says that before he got into the boat, Revere remembered that he had nothing with which to muffle his oars. None of the three men dared to go back into the Boston streets, but one had an idea. He turned toward a house on the bank of the river and whistled an unusual tune. A window in that house opened, and the man's girlfriend poked her head out. The man whispered, the girl disappeared, and soon a flannel petticoat was tossed into the man's waiting hands. Revere took this "oar muffler" gratefully. Another story says that Revere sent his faithful dog back home with a note asking his wife to send back the spurs he had forgotten. According to that story, the dog returned with the spurs tied around his collar.

As the men rowed across the Charles River, it seemed that the *Somerset* was blocking their way. But they managed to sneak by the big ship undetected and reach the Charlestown shore safely, where fellow Patriots were waiting for Revere. Among them was a colonel who assured Revere that the lanterns had been seen and the signal passed on by hundreds of Patriots. That was the good news. The bad news was that British officers were patrolling all the roads from Boston to Cambridge and on to Concord. Somehow, Revere would have to get by them. If any rider and horse could make it, they said, it was Paul Revere and Brown Beauty, his strong, sure-footed, and tireless horse.

Around eleven o'clock that night, Paul Revere swung up onto his horse and traveled as swiftly as he dared but not so feverishly as to attract the attention of a Redcoat guard. On this chilly night, the moon shone brightly. Revere could make out some familiar landmarks.

Revere's warning was not a complete surprise to the rebels along his way. Members of the Committees of Safety, the minutemen, and other spies had spread the word that the British had decided to stop the rebellion once and for all. The citizens along Revere's route already knew that the British were headed out of Boston. Now they awaited the all-important answer to the questions: When and where would they attack? Colonial soldiers and their officers prepared to defend their families and friends and their property. Riders waited to spread the news as soon as they received it. Townspeople made plans to light signal fires, ring church bells, and fire guns to further spread the alarm.

Moving more slowly but heading in the same direction as Revere were the British Regulars. For the first few miles, despite the physical discomfort, they were buoyed. They were proud to be the forces that would put down a rebellion against their king. The colonists refused to accept the fact that the Redcoats were representatives of the crown and should be treated with respect. For years, the Yankee patriots had made fun of the soldiers and harassed them mercilessly. Worse, the Patriots had declared that they did not have to obey the orders of the king or the Parliament. Whether these colonists were viewed as irresponsible British citizens or as traitors to the crown, it was clearly the duty of the king's soldiers to take any action necessary to bring peace and stability to this colony of the British Empire. They felt sure that this surprise attack, planned so well by General Thomas Gage, commander-in-chief of British forces in America and also governor of Boston, would establish the authority of Great Britain once and for all.

Chapter Seven

Paul Revere's Ride

The Regulars had not been marching along the deserted roads for long before they began to hear sounds that signaled trouble. At first, faintly in the distance and gradually closer and closer, the sounds of church bells and gun shots reached their ears. Soon it was obvious that Gage's planned surprise attack was no surprise at all. Somehow, Patriot spies had learned of the plans and had warned the citizens of Lexington, and maybe those of Concord, that the Redcoats were coming and they were on the search for munitions and other supplies as well as for traitors to the king.

British Colonel Francis Smith did not consider turning back. He sent an order for Major John Pitcairn to head for Lexington on the double. Then he continued his march to Concord.

As the Regulars made their way through the night, Patriot Captain John Parker, a veteran of the French and Indian War, drilled the militia assembled on Lexington Common in the dark and cold. He sent some scouts along the road toward Boston. The scouts returned, saying that they saw no sign of the British. Parker told the frustrated men that they could relax at Buckman's Tavern on the condition that they return on the double to the Common when called.

Meanwhile, Revere galloped toward the Reverend Jonas Clark's home in Lexington. He rode through Charlestown, speeding by the Charles River on his left and the Mystic River on his right. Suddenly in the darkness, he made out the holsters and helmet decorations of two British officers standing under a tree. Apparently the officers just as quickly recognized the stocky figure, who was well known as a fast and efficient messenger for the rebels. Revere wrote about what happened next: "One of them started his horse towards me, and the other up the road, as I supposed to head me [off] should I escape the first. I turned my horse about and rid upon a full gallop for Mistick Road." He quickly outdistanced the Redcoats.

Revere knew the route well, and he and Brown Beauty moved easily together. At times, his mind must have leaped ahead to the consequences if he were captured. One punishment for treason was drawing and quartering. He must have shaken away the thought because he had a job to do, and it had to be done quickly. He was forced to make a detour because the main road to Cambridge was blocked by Regulars. He crossed the plank bridge over to Medford and proceeded from there, spreading the alarm to minutemen at almost every house along the way.

Behind him the tumult rose—"The Regulars are coming out!" accompanied by tolling bells and beating drums. As soon as they heard these words, Patriots sprang into action. Some men grabbed muskets and rushed toward Concord. Others hid supplies in cellars, attics, and nearby woods. Women and children fled to hiding places in the swamps and woods. Some men offered to help spread the warning. Soon couriers were criss-crossing the area around Lexington and Charlestown.

It was midnight when Revere rode his exhausted horse into the Reverend Clark's yard in Lexington. He shouted to the watchmen, "The Regulars are coming out!" and dashed into the house to alert Adams and Hancock. Those two men were arguing about their next move. Hancock was cleaning his gun and sword, eager to take his place among the armed farmers. Adams was repeating, "It is not our business; we belong to the cabinet."

Dawes came in about half an hour later. After eating and drinking, he and Revere decided to head for Concord. They had accomplished their major task of alerting Hancock and Adams and had sent word to Concord to hide their weapons. Now, Revere wanted to go to Concord again to check on the situation and to warn any along the way who had not been informed of the coming British. As he and Dawes rode out of Lexington, they were joined by young Dr. Samuel Prescott, who offered to ride with them. The three men galloped through the darkness.

At one point, Revere went ahead while the other two

A patriotic depiction of Paul Revere's ride.

stopped at farmhouses. Suddenly he saw two British officers in front of him. He shouted a warning to Dawes and Prescott. Only Prescott was able to gallop away. Dawes fell off his horse and then somehow managed to escape on foot. The officers seized Revere's bridle, pointed their pistols at his chest and ordered him to dismount, saying, "If you go an inch further you are a dead man."

As Revere slid off his horse, he saw that he was not the only rebel captive. Four captured colonists were closely guarded by the officers. A major held his gun to Revere's head and demanded that he answer their questions truthfully. "If you attempt to run, or we are insulted, we will blow your brains out," he warned. Revere answered, "I will tell the truth, for I am not afraid." The officers asked Revere about the sound of alarm guns from Lexington. Revere answered that rebels all around the countryside had heard the alarm and were spreading the warning. He realized that his captors would have no way to know what was going on in Boston, so he told them that the Regulars' boats had gone aground. The militia would make the most of that delay, he said, and would have over 500 men waiting at Lexington. The Regulars quickly decided that they had no time to bother with prisoners; they needed to get to Lexington fast. They cut the bridles off the horses of all the prisoners but Revere. For several minutes more, they debated what to do with him. They finally decided that he would be more in their way than he was worth. They had to get to Lexington fast. They grabbed Brown Beauty, gave her to one of their soldiers, and then set Revere free also. The soldiers galloped off toward Lexington.

The Patriots who were freed earlier were making their way over stone walls and across pastures to Lexington Common. Revere went to the Reverend Clark's house, where he found Hancock and Adams still arguing about joining the fighting. Finally, around daybreak, Hancock was persuaded not to join the militia. He told the men of a potentially dangerous situation, the trunk full of papers that would easily incriminate him as a traitor. He worried that the British would find the trunk, which was in an upper floor of Buckman's Tavern on the Lexington Common. Revere promised to do what he could after he had accompanied the two "traitors" to a home near Woburn.

Along the way to Woburn, alerted citizens fanned out over the countryside into the areas they knew well. A few minutes after the three men arrived safely, Revere's curiosity got the better of him. He kept hearing conflicting reports about the British troops and plans, and he needed to check out the situation for himself. He agreed when Hancock's clerk, John Lowell, asked him to return to Lexington with him to get Hancock's trunk. They planned to hide it in Reverend Clark's parsonage.

As Revere and Lowell crossed the Common in the gray dawn, they saw militia gathering. Captain Parker had sent out a scout who returned saying that he had seen the Regulars approaching and that they were close. Parker had ordered a drum beat and warning shots to spread the message that the soldiers were to return to the Common. Fifteen minutes later they were lined up double file on the grounds behind the three-story high meeting house.

Historians debate the number of Patriot troops, some putting it as high as 130 and most reporting about sixty or seventy. Some say that the militia included nearly half the adult males in the town. They awaited orders from Captain Parker, stamping their feet and blowing on their hands to keep warm. Revere knew that he could not help them, so the two men made their way through the ranks to the tavern.

There they found Hancock's wooden chest, a heavy box four feet long and about two and a half feet high. Before they picked it up, they paused a moment at the window. Dawn was breaking, and they could make out the outlines of the militia. Then they saw the orderly ranks of Redcoats marching briskly along toward the Common. The sun glinted on their bayonets and on the perspiring backs of the officers' horses. Revere knew that nothing he could do to help the Patriots would be more important than hiding Hancock's papers, so he successfully secreted the trunk.

Six hundred Redcoats approached the Common in three orderly platoons. They stopped momentarily to load their muskets, then they continued toward the green. On Major Pitcairn's order to halt, the British soldiers stopped about 150 feet away from the Patriots. The Redcoats were still wet and cold from standing in the cold shallows of the Charles River. They were exhausted from their double-time trek through the Massachusetts countryside to Lexington. They were frustrated to have their surprise attack foiled. Above all, they were fed up with the Patriots who questioned their right to even be in Massachusetts. The two groups stood and stared at each other.

The Regulars may have expected a much stronger enemy than the handful of Patriots facing them. After all, the Patriots had been ringing church bells and firing warning shots to sound the alarm. And what kind of soldiers were they, this regiment of seventy men between the ages of sixteen and seventy? Most wore their farmer's large hats with floppy brims, breeches fastened just below the knee, long stockings, and cowhide shoes with large buckles. Their coats were of many different colors, as were their vests. Some carried long hunting rifles called "fowlers,"

Major Pitcairn's British troops commanded Lexington Common after the Patriot militia ran for cover. *(Courtesy of the Connecticut Historical Society, Hartford.)*

some had shorter muskets, some had antique guns. Most carried their precious lead bullets wrapped in handker-chiefs and their gunpowder stored in horns. A few carried short, century-old swords. Others carried no weapon at all. To complete the strange scene, the women and children of Lexington watched from the doors and windows of build-ings around the Common.

Revere and Lowell passed through the militia, lugging the trunk. As Revere passed by Captain Parker, he heard the officer order: "Let the troops pass by, don't molest them unless they begin first."

Pitcairn ordered his men: "On no account will you fire, or even attempt it without orders." Then he and two officers galloped toward the militia. Pitcairn shouted to the Patri-ots: "Ye villains, ye rebels, disperse! Damn you, disperse!"

There was no answer. Other British officers shouted the same warning.

As Revere and Lowell walked away from the green, they heard a shot. There are many stories and legends about what happened next. The only verified fact is that there was gunfire, and there were soon injuries and deaths. British Major John Pitcairn later insisted that he had not given his soldiers the order to fire. One widely-held belief is that some other British officer had shouted "fire, damn you, fire," and that the Regulars then rushed in with blazing guns and bayonets ready to charge.

The next proven facts are that both sides skirmished for about ten minutes before the militia soldiers ran for cover.

Eight Americans were killed, and ten wounded. Captain Parker was wounded by a gunshot and then finished off with a bayonet. One story says that Pitcairn drove his horse in among his men, cursing them for firing the first shot. One report says that a single British soldier was slightly wounded. It is known that the militia retreated in confusion. Another legend reports that Sam Adams, then on the way to Woburn, heard the shots and exclaimed, "Oh, what a glorious morning is this!"

Just moments later, British Colonel Francis Smith arrived with his main body of troops. Drummers sounded the command to form regiments. The troops cheered and fired a victory salute as they marched out of Lexington and on to Concord.

Before nightfall on that day, over 4,000 American militia would see action. Seventy-three British soldiers would be killed; ninety-three American soldiers would be either killed, wounded, or missing. On that nineteenth day of April in 1775, the American Revolutionary War would begin.

Chapter Eight

On to Concord

Residents in Concord had heard the alarm. They had removed most of the military supplies to safety. A farmer plowed furrows over the hastily buried cannon in his field. A woman hid the church silver in a barrel of soap. Others found their own special hiding places around their farms and fields. Early that Wednesday morning, they did not yet know that eight of their countrymen had been killed in Lexington, but they were armed and, they hoped, ready for whatever might happen. The militia kept watch from Punkatassett Hill overlooking the North Bridge, where they expected to see the first signs of the Redcoats.

The alarm had reached far and wide. Minutemen rushed in from the neighboring counties of Worcester and Hampshire and later arrived from as far away as New Hampshire and Maine. All around Concord, wives filled pillowcases with a loaf of bread, a hunk of salt beef, and an extra pair of stockings to give to their husbands as they kissed them goodbye.

On their high point about a mile from town, the militia watched as the Redcoats entered Concord, their weapons glistening in the morning sun. British Captain Walter Laurie was left with a detachment of about 100 men to guard the Concord Bridge while the others invaded the town. Historians differ about what the other Regulars did next. Some reports say that the Redcoats immediately committed atrocities on citizens as they passed by homes. Others say that the Redcoats hurt no one but ransacked kitchens and pantries for food. It is known that they threw 500 Patriot musket balls into a pond and burned a Liberty Pole. Smoke from this fire, which spread to a courthouse roof, alerted the militia reinforcements, who speeded their march to the bridge.

Nervous, Captain Laurie sent for reinforcements. Major Pitcairn sat in a tavern refreshing himself, relishing the success at Lexington, and looking forward to the same kind of success in Concord. Colonel Francis Smith received Laurie's message, but he did not hurry. Today, historians wonder what might have happened if Smith had been quicker to act. As it happened, Smith arrived in the center of Concord and marched his men back and forth to pass the time as he waited for Lord Hugh Percy and his troops to join him so they could arrive at the North Bridge together.

In the meantime, Patriot Major John Buttrick ordered his 500-man militia to advance toward the British Regulars at the other end of the narrow bridge. They obeyed, parading briskly down the hill to the fife and drum tune of "The White

Cockade," determined to win or to die in the attempt. Laurie knew he did not have time to wait for the reinforcements. He ordered his men to pull up the planks on the bridge to stop the militia, but he was not quick enough. The 500 Americans marched steadily onto the bridge, stopping when they saw about eighty British Regulars in their bright red uniforms facing them.

At the other end of the bridge, British Captain Walter Laurie hoped that the British Brown Bess guns would somehow make up for the difference in numbers. A Brown Bess was a musket about four-and-a half feet long that fired three-quarter inch balls. If a soldier were within 125 yards of his target, he could point and shoot Brown Bess with some confidence of hitting his target.

Laurie probably considered firing the first shot at the North Bridge, but he did not do it. Nobody knows who did, but records show that it was fired from the British side. That first bullet splashed in the river. A fraction of a second later, perhaps twenty more British bullets flew toward the Patriots. Three of these shots hit their mark: Two militia men were struck dead, and one was wounded.

"God damn it," shouted a militia captain, "they are firing ball." Major Buttrick gave the order, "Fire, fellow soldiers! For God's sake, fire!" In that first round of shooting, the colonists killed three men and wounded four officers. This marked the first instance in which the Americans deliberately attacked the king's forces. This offensive action, in contrast to previous armed conflicts where the colonists

Colonel Smith and Major Pitcairn at the cemetary above Concord.

had acted defensively, became celebrated as "the shot heard round the world" in Ralph Waldo Emerson's poem, "Concord Hymn."

With overpowering numbers and excellent marksmanship, the colonists soon drove the British off the bridge. In just five minutes, the British were retreating. The Americans rushed across the bridge and lay in ambush, ready to fire on any Redcoat who returned or did not retreat swiftly enough. Other Patriots joined them. Soon the hills around the bridge were covered with rebels, 3,000 of them, and they kept a steady stream of fire on the road. Exhausted and fearful, British soldiers scrambled to get away from the rapid fire of the militia. Most Redcoats had used all their rounds of ammunition. Now their Brown Bess muskets seemed to be a major disadvantage because they took a long time to load. A soldier had to bite off the end of a paper cartridge containing the powder and the ball. Then he shook some powder into the firing pan of his gun, rested the butt of his musket on the ground, poured the powder and the ball into the barrel, and rammed in a wad of paper to hold the shot in place. When he pulled the trigger, the firing cock fell, and the flint struck steel, causing a spark that ignited the powder in the firing pan. The ball was sent flying. A competent marksman could get off fifteen shots in four minutes, and then he had to re-load.

The British soldiers panicked, knowing they were un-able to defend themselves in retreat as they hurried back to Boston. All along the twelve miles to the city, Patriots sniped at them from farm walls, from behind hedges, from windows and roofs, keeping up a steady fire. A British officer wrote later: "We marched between nine and ten miles, [the rebels'] numbers increasing from all parts, while ours were reducing by deaths, wounds and fatigue . . ." When they arrived back in Boston, the British made a quick count. Seventy-three of their men had been killed and another 200 wounded. They learned later that the Ameri-cans had ninety-three casualties.

The Patriot offensive in Lexington and Concord set off an alarm that rang through the colonies, a cry for indepen-dence at any cost. Although no one will ever know who fired that first shot, almost everyone agrees that it was that blast

The British were forced to retreat from Concord on April 19, 1775.

from a British musket that started the colonists' war for independence. That shot ended any opportunity for mediation, negotiation, or any other attempt to talk of peace. The Revolutionary War had begun.

Within the next few days, militiamen were called to defend their rights throughout the countryside. Riders galloped from farm to farm and church bells rang, calling the men to arms. Dr. Joseph Warren sent out a call to enlist: "An hour lost may deluge your country in blood and entail perpetual slavery upon the few of your posterity who may survive the carnage." Gage found himself surrounded by more than 10,000 rebels, poorly equipped and scarcely prepared, but ready to die for their cause.

Less than a month after the battles of Concord and Lexington, the Second Continental Congress met in Philadelphia. Delegates from every colony (except Georgia, who joined the congress a few months later) gathered in the Pennsylvania statehouse, an impressive brick building with a white steeple. A single glance at the building showed the dilemma of the delegates gathered there. The bell in the steeple spoke for the rebels with its engraved message: "Proclaim liberty throughout all the land unto all the inhabitants thereof." The main entrance spoke for the crown with its large copy of the coat of arms of George III. The representatives voted for independence at any cost.

While the congress was meeting, the British declared that Boston was under martial law. A few days later, the famous battles of Breed's and Bunker Hill took place. American General Israel Putnam, needing to conserve ammunition, told his troops: "Don't fire until you see the whites of their eyes." The Americans ran out of ammunition by five o'clock in the afternoon. The British won the battle, but with over 1,000 casualties to the Americans' 400 casualties. Two weeks later, the Continental Congress took control of the militia and established an army of 20,000 soldiers under Commander-in-Chief George Washington.

Sam Adams continued to fight for independence, but he did not join the military. Although he was elected each year

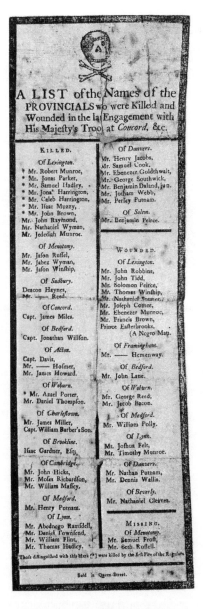

The American dead at Concord.

to the Massachusetts House of Representatives, he spent little time with the group as a whole. He tended to work alone, trying to convince other representatives, one at a time, to agree with his positions and to vote with him.

When he was elected to the Continental Congress, Sam Adams also worked hard to persuade his colleagues to agree with his opinions. He worked to pass legislation to authorize procurement of supplies for an additional army of 23,000 men. He and John Hancock began to see less and less of each other. Their differences had arisen during the time when Sam Adams urged boycotts against English goods. As an importer, Hancock had lost a great deal of money because of his patriotism and siding with Adams. Their differences had grown when Sam Adams supported congressional delegate George Washington for commander-in-chief of the American armies. Hancock wanted that position for himself.

Perhaps another reason was the great difference in their lifestyles. Hancock drove to congressional meetings in an elegant coach. Sam Adams walked. Hancock ate at the best inns in town. Adams preferred simple meals at common taverns. Hancock was talked about all over town for his fancy clothes. Sam Adams scarcely had a change of clothes from day to day.

Both Adams and Hancock signed the Declaration of Independence, which was adopted on July 4, 1776. After that signing, Adams had much less to do with the fate of the new country. He had done the work he knew best: He had

General George Washington was appointed commander-in-chief of the new American army.

helped to start a successful revolution. He would leave the jobs of building the military forces and, ultimately, forming a new government, to those who had more intuition and skill in such matters. Both Sam Adams and John Hancock served as governor of Massachusetts, Adams from 1794-97, and Hancock from 1780-85 and 1787-93.

Chapter Nine

A "Common Hero"

Heroes of the Revolution—Sam Adams, John Adams, Paul Revere, Dr. Joseph Warren, George Hewes . . .

George who? Hewes was a typical unsung hero who might have lived and died without a mention in any history books except that he was a storyteller. When Hewes told stories, people listened and remembered. In the 1830s, one of the people who listened was Benjamin B. Thatcher, who found Hewes's stories so fascinating that he wrote a biography of this shoemaker, military veteran, and proud revolutionary Patriot. Thatcher did not mind that Hewes probably tweaked some of his stories here and there to come out the way he wanted them to. He and Hewes made a good pair. Thatcher was looking for information about common men who were heroes of the Revolution. Hewes was looking for an audience to tell his revolution stories to.

George Robert Twelves Hewes was born in Boston in 1742. No one watching George grow up would suspect that an author would one day write his biography. He was one of nine children (four siblings died in infancy) born to a shoemaker and his wife. George grew up like many sons of tradesmen in Boston. He spent more time running errands for the family business than he did going to school.

George did not like school much anyway. He was much more interested in playing around the harbor and shipyards. He ran away from one school twice. He remembered little of the next school except that he was beaten with a switch every time he ran away. When his mother declared that she could no longer handle him, he was sent to his uncle's farm where he continued to be described as saucy and impudent.

Both his parents died when he was about thirteen. It was time for George to become an apprentice and learn a trade. Full of energy and a lover of action, George's first choice for a career was to build houses or ships. But he was just barely over five feet tall and would never have the strength for such work. Without family financial backing, he could not become an apprentice to one of the more lucrative trades such as blacksmithing or tanning or silversmithing. So, fourteen-year-old George entered one of the least desirable trades of all—shoemaking. For a while he stuck with this sedentary job, subject to frequent whipping from his master, who had no patience for this young boy with an attitude.

Then Hewes saw a way out of this despised existence. He would do what some other young men did when they were unhappy with their lives: He would enlist. The British army, stationed in Boston, often sent recruiters drumming through the streets looking for enlistees. George was told by the recruiter that he missed the height requirement by a little more than an inch.

Not defeated, George went to a friend's shoe shop and had taps put on his shoes. He returned to the recruiting center. His trick was soon found out, and he was rejected again.

He then went to the wharf and tried to enlist on a British warship. His brothers put an end to this plan. They had heard that life on a British ship was like life in a prison, and they refused to allow him to volunteer.

He returned to shoemaking and built a shop where he worked for several years. He married and had many children, probably eleven of whom survived infancy.

His work was mostly making custom shoes and repairing shoes and boots. No records of his work remain, but since he lived in a poorer section of town, it is assumed that his customers were mostly poor. In any case, two years after his marriage he was put in debtor's prison. Records do not show how he obtained his release. He went back to work and stayed poor. The boycott of imports in 1767 might have helped him. But it appears that shoemakers from nearby Lynn captured most of the trade that had formerly gone to importers.

For many years, Hewes did not belong to groups and clubs. He was not even a taxpayer because he did not own enough property. When his friends and relatives began to attend town meetings to protest the authority of the crown, Hewes did not join them. He simply did not care.

Then a British sentry challenged him when he was out after the curfew. All of a sudden, Hewes did care—very much—about the authority of the crown. He was further irritated when a British soldier cheated him. The Redcoat ordered and took a pair of shoes and then did not pay. Hewes's anger rose in February 1770 when an eleven-year-old schoolboy, picketing against imported goods, was shot and killed. He reacted in anger again when British soldiers and American workers battled because the soldiers were trying to earn money by taking part-time jobs. He was still more embittered at the scene of an ugly confrontation between ropewalk workers and British soldiers who were looking for part-time work in the maritime trade.

On the evening of the Boston Massacre, Hewes heard the shouting on King Street, and he went there to see what was going on. One glance at the snowballs and ice being thrown and the threatening clubs and sticks, and Hewes "was soon on the ground among them," he told his biographer. He was standing next to James Caldwell, a ship's mate, when Caldwell was shot. Hewes helped carry him to a doctor. Hewes said afterward that he believed that the Americans had every right to refuse to leave King Street because it was a public highway.

That memory of the Boston Massacre stayed in Hewes's mind, and he was a changed man from that time on. He could not forget the scene of thousands of angry townspeople facing British soldiers and their rifles. In the days afterward, Hewes went to the town meetings at Old South

A crowd of angry Bostonians rebels against the crown by burning printed materials that were subject to taxation under the Stamp Act.

Church. At these meetings, anyone, property holder or not, was allowed to vote, and Hewes voted to send officials to the governor to demand that British troops be removed from Boston.

After the meeting, he headed home to arm himself. On the way, a British soldier seized Hewes's cane and would not give it back. Hewes was stirred to stronger political action. He was one of almost 100 Bostonians who gave a deposition describing what he had seen at the Massacre. Hewes told his biographer that he testified at the trial of Captain Preston and that he swore that Preston had given the order to fire. Historians are not sure if he really did testify or not. But they say that his memory, faulty or not, shows that George Hewes was deeply involved in the conflict. He had become more than a struggling shoemaker. He had become a member of that large group of "common" people now referred to in history books generically as citizens of Boston, Patriots, and rebels.

Four years later, Hewes said he was involved in the Boston Tea Party. He told his biographer that he disguised himself as an Indian and rubbed coal dust on his hands and face. Then he joined the others who were marching toward Griffin's Wharf. When they arrived at the wharf, they were assigned to three different groups. Hewes, a follower up until this time, became a leader. He was asked by his commander to approach the captain of the ship and demand the keys to the hatches and some candles. The captain complied.

In an act of defiance against unfair British policies toward the colonies, Bostonians hoist a government official up a Liberty Pole.

When all the tea was floating in the harbor, the men prepared to leave the ship. Hewes saw that one of the "Indians" had stuffed his pockets and coat lining with tea. Hewes threatened him but was unable to catch him as he ran down the wharf.

No one knows how many thousands of Americans were, like Hewes, mostly undisturbed by the British military presence until specific incidents goaded them into action. He was personally insulted when a British soldier questioned him about being out after the curfew. He was outraged when he saw an eleven-year-old boy shot and killed by soldiers. His temper rose when British soldiers tried to take jobs from Boston civilians. He did not want to pay a tax on tea. When faced with these affronts, Hewes and many like him became committed enemies of Britain.

Historians sometimes define a "common" man as one who is not a member of any organized committee or club, one who acts of his own will without waiting for the call of a leader, and one who can volunteer and assume leadership. Hewes fits this definition by his avoidance of groups like the Sons of Liberty, his actions at the Boston Massacre, and his leadership at the Boston Tea Party.

Without Hewes and so-called "commoners" like him, John Adams, Sam Adams, Paul Revere, Dr. Joseph Warren, and other famous patriots could not have succeeded.

Appendix

Famous Leaders

Adams, John: John Adams was inaugurated the second president of the United States of America on March 4, 1797. He lost his bid for re-election in 1800. Adams died on July 4, 1826, the fiftieth anniversary of the Declaration of Independence.

Adams, Samuel: Sam Adams helped to draft the Massachusetts State Constitution. He was governor of Massachusetts from 1794-97.

Bernard, Francis: After Governor Bernard was recalled to England in 1769, he was made a baron. Bernard died in England in 1779, two years before the British surrender at Yorktown.

Gage, Thomas: Gage was appointed commander-in-chief of all British forces in America in August 1775. He resigned from that position two months later and returned to England.

George III: King George III was suspected of suffering from dementia around 1765. He continued to show signs of mental problems until his death in 1820.

Hancock, John: Hancock was the first member of the Continental Congress to sign the Declaration of Independence. He served as governor of Massachusetts until his death in 1789.

Henry, Patrick: Henry was governor of Virginia in 1776-79 and 1784-86. He was pivotal in the adoption of the first ten amendments to the Constitution, called the Bill of Rights.

Hutchinson, Thomas: After returning to England in 1774, Governor Hutchinson was awarded an honorary doctorate of civil law.

Jefferson, Thomas: Jefferson was president from 1801-08. A major focus of his administration was encouragement of westward expansion and exploration.

Thomas, Isaiah: Thomas printed more than 400 books including a Bible, educational material, and children's books. He founded the American Antiquarian Society to preserve materials for the study of American history.

Revere, Paul: After the war, Revere went back to his successful business as a silversmith.

Washington, George: Washington was inaugurated as first president of the United States of America in 1789. He served two terms and then declined a third term.

Glossary

Boston Common—A park-like area near the center of Boston used for grazing and sometimes as a site for informal and formal meetings.

Circular Letter—A letter that was sent from colony to colony.

Committee of Correspondence—Group formed to report developments in the struggle between Britain and the colonies. By 1774, every colony had an active Committee of Correspondence.

congress—A formal assembly of representatives.

Loyalist—An English citizen who remained loyal to the British crown during the hostilities with America.

Massachusetts General Court—Legislature of the state of Massachusetts.

minutemen—Militia formed in Massachusetts over the winter of 1774-75 to defend against British troops.

musket—A shoulder gun used in the late sixteenth through the eighteenth centuries.

Parliament—The national legislature of England consisting of the House of Lords and the House of Commons.

quarter—To furnish with housing.

Regular—A British soldier in America.

treason—Violation of allegiance toward one's country.

Chapter Notes

CHAPTER ONE

p. 10, "[T]he multitude was shouting . . ." Miller, John C.,
Sam Adams: Pioneer in Propaganda. Stanford:
Stanford University Press, 1936, p. 179.

p. 14, "Lobster back, I'm going to have . . ." Tebbell, John.
Turning the World Upside Down. New York: Orion
Books,1993, p. 17.

CHAPTER TWO

p. 18, "Innocence is no longer safe . . ." Miller, op.cit., p.
192.

p. 18, "I have a dread of contempt . . ." Fritz, Jean. *Cast for
a Revolution.* Boston: Houghton Mifflin Company,
1972, p. 71.

p. 18, "stiff and uneasy . . ." Bailyn, Bernard. *Faces of
Revolution.* New York: Alfred A. Knopf, 1990, p. 8.

p. 18, "I am resolved to rise . . ." Bailyn, op.cit., p. 6.

p. 20, "Our British ancestors . . ." Forbes, Esther. *Paul
Revere & the World He Lived In.* Boston: Houghton
Mifflin Company, 1942, p. 83.

CHAPTER THREE

p. 28, "I hope the same spirit . . ." Wagner, Frederick. *Patriot's Choice: The Story of John Hancock*. New York: Dodd, Mead & Company, 1964, p. 39.

p. 31, "to make united and successful . . ." Forbes, op.cit., p. 182.

p. 32, "This meeting can do no more . . ." Hibbert, Christopher. *Redcoats and Rebels*. New York: W.W. Norton & Company, 1990, p. 20.

CHAPTER FOUR

p. 34, "convince your colonies . . ." Triber, Jayne. *A True Republican: The Life of Paul Revere*. Amherst: University of Massachusetts, 1998, p. 97.

p. 35, "the foulest, subtlest, and most venomous . . . " Davidson, James W. and Mark H. Lytle. *The United States: A History of the Republic*. New Jersey: Prentice-Hall, Inc., 1981, p. 112.

p. 36, "Our oppressors cannot force us . . ." Langguth, A.J. *Patriots: The Men Who Started the American Revolution*. New York: Simon and Schuster, 1988, p. 201.

p. 36, "If this be treason . . ." op.cit., p. 69.

p. 42, "It is a curious masquerade . . ." Fischer, David H. *Paul Revere's Ride*. New York: Oxford University Press, 1994, p. 154.

p. 45, "blows must decide . . ." Davidson, op.cit., p.122.

p. 45, "[F]orce should be repelled . . ." Cook, Don. *The Long Fuse*. New York: The Atlantic Monthly Press, 1995, p. 211.

p. 48, " 'Put your enemy in the wrong' . . ." Fischer, op.cit., p. 79.

CHAPTER FIVE

p. 49, "If our Trade be taxed . . ." Miller, John C..op.cit., p. 45.

p. 51, "so they might have no pretence . . ." Forbes, op.cit., p. 229.

p. 52, "I glory in publicly avowing . . ." Wagner, op.cit., p. 100.

p. 58, "if the British went out by water . . ." Forbes, op.cit., p. 238.

CHAPTER SEVEN

p. 71, "One of them started his horse . . ." Ibid., p. 248.

p. 72, "It is not our business . . ." Ibid., p. 254.

p. 73, "If you go an inch further . . ." Ibid., p. 251.

p. 73, "If you attempt to run . . ." Fischer, op.cit., p. 134.

p. 78, "Let the troops pass by . . ." Tebbell, op.cit., p. 46.

p. 78, "On no account . . . " Ibid.

p. 78, "Ye villains, ye rebels . . ."Ibid.

p. 78, "fire, damn you, fire" Hibbert, op.cit.., p. 32.

p. 79, "Oh, what a glorious morning . . ." McDowell, Bart. *The Revolutionary War.* Washington, D.C.: National Geographic Society, 1967, p. 43.

CHAPTER EIGHT

p. 82, "God damn it! . . ." Langguth, op.cit., p. 245.

p. 82, "Fire, fellow soldiers!" Ibid.

p. 83, "the shot heard round the world," McDowell, op.cit.,
p. 47.

p. 84, "We marched between nine and ten miles . . ."
Hibbert, op.cit., p. 34.

p. 85, "An hour lost may deluge your country . . ." Langguth,
op.cit., p. 252.

p. 86, "Proclaim liberty throughout . . ." Davidson, op.cit.,
p. 119.

p. 86, "Don't fire until you see . . ." Ibid.

CHAPTER NINE

p. 94, "was soon on the ground . . ." Young, Alfred F. *The
Shoemaker and the Tea Party*. Boston: Beacon Press,
1999, p. 38.

.

Bibliography

Bailyn, Bernard. *Faces of Revolution*. New York: Alfred A. Knopf, 1990.

Bobrick, Benson. *Angel in the Whirlwind*. New York: Simon & Schuster, 1997.

Canfield, Cass. *Sam Adams's Revolution*. New York: Harper & Row, 1976.

Davidson, James W. and Mark H. Lytle, *The United States: A History of the Republic*. New Jersey: Prentice- Hall, Inc., 1981.

Fischer, David H. *Paul Revere's Ride*. New York: Oxford University Press, 1994.

Fleming, Thomas. *Liberty! The American Revolution*. New York: Viking, 1997.

Forbes, Esther. *Paul Revere & the World He Lived In.* Boston: Houghton Mifflin Company, 1942.

Fritz, Jean. *Cast for a Revolution.* Boston: Houghton Mifflin Company, 1972.

Hall, Michael, Lawrence Leder and Michael Kammen, eds. *The Glorious Revolution in America.* Chapel Hill: The University of North Carolina Press, 1964.

Hibbert, Christopher. *Redcoats and Rebels.* New York: W.W. Norton & Company, 1990.

Ketchum, Richard (ed.) *American Heritage Book of the Revolution.* New York: American Heritage Publishing Co., Inc., 1958.

Lukes, Bonnie L. *John Adams: Public Servant.* Greensboro, N.C., Morgan Reynolds Publishers, 2001.

McDowell, Bart. *The Revolutionary War.* Washington, D.C., National Geographic Society, 1967.

Miller, John C. *Origins of the American Revolution.* California: Stanford University Press, 1943.
———. *Sam Adams: Pioneer in Propaganda.* Stanford: Stanford University Press, 1936.

Triber, Jayne. *A True Republican: The Life of Paul Revere.* Amherst: University of Massachusetts, 1998.

Vaughan, Alden T., ed. *Chronicles of the American Revolution.* New York: Grosset & Dunlap, 1965.

Wagner, Frederick. *Patriot's Choice: The Story of John Hancock.* New York: Dodd, Mead & Company, 1964.

Young, Alfred F. *The Shoemaker and the Tea Party.* Boston: Beacon Press, 1999.

Index

Adams, Abigail, 22

Adams, John, 10, 18, 20, 22-23, *25*, 36, 49, 55, 91, 98

Adams, Samuel, 15-16, *17*, 18, 22-24, 26, 30-32, 36, 46, 48-49, 51-52, 54-55, 57-58, 60, 64, 66, 72, 74, 79, 86, 88, 90-91, 98

Attucks, Crispus, 12, 14

Barrett, James, 54

Bentley, Joshua, 67

Boston Massacre, *13*, 15, 18, 24, 50-52, 55, 94, 96-98

Boston Tea Party, 32, *33*, 34, 57, 96-98

Breed's Hill, Battle of, 86

Brown Beauty, 68, 71, 74

Bunker Hill, Battle of, 86

Buttrick, John, 81-82

Caldwell, James, 94

Clark, Jonas, 71-72, 74-75

Committees of Correspondence, 22, 24, 31, 35

Committees of Safety, 38, 68

Concord, Battle of, 80-82, *83*, 84, *85*

"Concord Hymn," 83

Dartmouth, 30-31

Dartmouth, William, 45

Dawes, William, 63-64, *65*, 72-73

Declaration of Independence, 88
Declaration and Resolves, 36
Dickenson, John, 36

East India Company, 26
Emerson, Ralph Waldo, 83

Faneuil Hall, 31
First Continental Congress, 36, 38
Franklin, Benjamin, 46
French and Indian War, 38, 70

Gage, Thomas, 33-35, 42, *43*, 44-45, 50, 52, 55-56, 58, 63, 69-70, 85
Galloway, Joseph, 36
Garrick, Edward, 10
George III, King of England, 9, 33, 44-46, *47*, 48, 51, 86
Green Dragon Tavern, 42, 48-49

Hancock, John, 27-28, *29*, 48-49, 51, 54-55, 57, 60, 64, 66, 72, 74-76, 88, 90
Harvard College, 16
Hatcher, Benjamin B., 91
Henry, Patrick, 36, 39
Hewes, George, 91-93, 96-98
Howe, John, 54-55
Hutchinson, Thomas, 14, 16, 18, *19*, 22, 30, 32, 35

Intolerable Acts (Coercive Acts), 34-35

Laurie, Walter, 81-82
Lexington, Battle of, 76, *77*, 78-79
Liberty, 28
Liberty Tree, 21, 31, *37*
Lowell, John, 75-78

Massachussetts Provincial Congress, 38

Navigation Acts, 15
Newman, Robert, 58, 66
North, Frederick, 26-28, 30, 33-34, *41*, 46

Parker, John, 70-71, 75, 78-79

Percy, Hugh, 81

Pitcairn, John, 70, 76, *77*, 78-79, 81, *83*

Prescott, Samuel, 72-73

Preston, Thomas, 12, 14, 22-23, 96

Pullings, John, 66

Putnam, Israel, 86

Quartering Act, 15, 63

Revere, Paul, 24, 31, 42, 57-58, *59*, 60, 63-64, 66-67, 71-72, *73*, 74-76, 78, 91, 98

Richardson, Thomas, 67

Romney, 28

Second Continental Congress, 55, 86, 88

Smith, Francis, 54-55, 63, 70, 79, 81, *83*

Sommerset, 60, 62-63, 66-67

Sons of Liberty, 16, 20, 22, 26-27, 30, 50, 98

Stamp Act, 15, 20

Tea Acts, 15

Thomas, Isaiah, 50

Thomson, Charles, 36

Townshend Acts, 23

Viscount Hillsborough, 45

Warren, Joseph, 51-52, *53*, 54, 63-64, 66, 85, 91, 98

Washington, George, 86, 88

"The White Cockade," 81

White, Hugh, 9-10